Heritage Lines
The Final Years

IAN BUCK

Key Books

BRITAIN'S RAILWAYS SERIES, VOLUME 49

Front cover image: Running on the Marston Valley line between Bedford and Bletchley, set 117704 arrives at Woburn Sands on 17 February 1999.

Title page image: A trio of Heritage diesel multiple units (DMUs) await an uncertain future at Tyseley Depot in February 1995.

Contents page image: Lasting well into the privatisation era, Class 121 no. 55032 is seen at Cardiff Queen Street in service with Arriva on the Cardiff Bay shuttle on 24 October 2007.

Back cover image: Class 101 cars 56062 and 51228 are seen in preservation with the North Norfolk Railway at Sheringham on 16 February 2022. Both were amongst the last cars to be withdrawn from the Manchester area.

Published by Key Books
An imprint of Key Publishing Ltd
PO Box 100
Stamford
Lincs PE9 1XQ

www.keypublishing.com

The right of Ian Buck to be identified as the author of this book has been asserted in accordance with the Copyright, Designs and Patents Act 1988 Sections 77 and 78.

Copyright © Ian Buck, 2023

ISBN 978 1 80282 672 2

All rights reserved. Reproduction in whole or in part in any form whatsoever or by any means is strictly prohibited without the prior permission of the Publisher.

Typeset by SJmagic DESIGN SERVICES, India.

Contents

Introduction 4

Chapter 1   Scotrail Survivors 6

                Trains to Whifflet 9

                Motherwell to Cumbernauld 11

                The Fife Circle 14

Chapter 2   The Far West to St Ives 17

Chapter 3   North London Variety 22

                The West London Line 22

                The Gospel Oak to Barking Line (the 'Goblin') 30

                The Marston Vale Line 41

                Loans and Off The Beaten Track 46

                Bletchley TMD 48

Chapter 4   Manchester's Mechanicals 52

                South Manchester 53

                Gogledd Cymru a Dyffryn Conwy/North Wales and the Conwy Valley 67

                North West 73

                Longsight TMD 79

Chapter 5   Storage and Disposal 82

Chapter 6   Departmental Units 91

Introduction

Imagine travelling in a train carriage full of fumes from the heater, vibrations from the engines, rattling windows dripping in condensation, the internal fug caused by damp clothing from the wet weather and a scene of urban decay outside the window. Believe it or not, I have just described a local train journey in the suburbs of North London or South Manchester at the end of the last century, creeping just into the 21st century with the last journey of this kind running until 2003!

At the beginning of the 1990s, the UK's National Network (previously British Rail [BR]) railways were stuck in limbo. BR had undertaken a large amount of modernisation in the later 1980s, but funding crises and the unknowns associated with looming privatisation of 1994 meant pockets of the 'old' railway lingered on for far longer than they should have done.

One of those pockets were the last remaining 'Heritage' diesel multiple units (DMUs), which ran on little-known and little-used services, often in the hearts of some of our greatest cities, and attempted to keep local trains running. Heritage DMU was a catch-all phrase that came to describe any of the diesel mechanical diesel multiple units that were in the class group of 1XX, which came about largely as a result of BR's 1955 modernisation plan. Some of these units lived long lives, with the last of the Class 101s surviving to almost 50 years old, and, even following withdrawal, many went straight into preservation.

In April 1994, the BR fleet of passenger rolling stock fleet were vested in three shadow Rolling Stock Companies (ROSCOs), and all of the Heritage DMUs were put into one ROSCO whether they were operational or not. With this in mind, April 1994 serves as a good starting point for this book. Sharp-eyed readers will note that the last two years of service (2002/3) are missing from this text – in 2001, I began working abroad and therefore missed the final days of these units.

I plan to give an overview of what happened as 2001 approached, list what was still running and where it ran, given from the perspective of one who was intrinsically involved with the fleet at this time. In the 1990s, I returned to working with these units as I had previous experience of them when they were operating the Reading to Gatwick services on the North Downs Line, and I even commuted to school on them in the early '70s when I lived in West London. They are a type of vehicle close to my heart, and I still try to travel on them in preservation whenever I can.

A number of vehicle types have been used throughout this book:

DMBS	Driving Motor Brake Standard
DMS	Driving Motor Standard
DMSL	Driving Motor Standard Lavatory
DTSL	Driving Trailer Standard Lavatory
TS	Trailer Standard
Power twin	A two-car unit with both cars powered
Motor	A car usually powered by two x diesel engines with driving cab
Brake	Provision for guard's brake van
Driving trailer	Unpowered car with driving cab
Trailer	Unpowered car without driving cab

It would be prudent at this stage to give a brief description of each class of DMU that appears in this book.

Introduction

Class 101 — This was a large fleet of vehicles built by Metropolitan Cammell of Birmingham between 1956 and 1960. Built with 57ft 6in bodies, they eventually operated on all BR regions. Train formations were varied, ranging from two-car to four-car, with some of the two-car units having driving trailers. All centre cars in the three- and four-car units were trailers. This was the last fleet in service, running until 2003, and many have survived in preservation.

Class 104 — Manufactured by the Birmingham Railway Carriage and Wagon Company between 1957 and 1959, this large fleet was built in two- and three-car formations. Spending their early lives in the Manchester and Hull areas, they were closely associated with the Manchester to Blackpool line. As withdrawals took place, some made their way south to operate lines around London, where the last were in use in 1993.

Class 116 — Built by BR at Derby Works between 1957 and 1958 to suburban design with 64ft bodies, this class of 3-car units started life on the Western Region and was most closely associated with the South Wales Valleys routes. The last few vehicles just made it into the privatisation era and were based at Tyseley, but very few have entered preservation.

Class 117 — Forty-three three-car sets were constructed by Pressed Steel Co Ltd in 1960 primarily for operating Paddington suburban services. They were built to the standard BR Derby suburban style and were very similar to Class 116s. They operated on the Western Region almost all their lives, until the introduction of the Networker Turbo units in the early 1990s meant their transfer to Scotrail and North London duties. Those in North London lost their trailer cars and operated as power twins. There was a small residual fleet also operating in the West Country. Their late withdrawal and lack of blue asbestos allowed many to go into preservation.

Class 119 — Gloucester Railway Carriage and Wagon Company (GRC&W) produced a number of three-car cross country sets for the Western Region in 1958 and 1959. They were built to quite a high standard, even including buffet cars. As time went on, they found themselves at Reading, where they operated the new Reading to Gatwick Airport service. The buffet area was converted into extra luggage space. After operation ceased on this route, the odd vehicle found its way into the Tyseley fleet with most of the others scrapped. Blue asbestos content meant only a few made it into preservation.

Class 121 — Pressed Steel produced 14 vehicles in 1960 that were effectively single-car versions of Class 117s. They found use mainly on London-area branches and in the West Country, with some making it latterly into the Birmingham area. Their versatility saw many end up in departmental service, and a few even made a comeback with train operators Arriva and Chiltern, becoming the last Heritage DMUs to operate on the network. Many have been preserved.

Class 122 — Another product of GRC&W, this small fleet of 20 single-car units was produced in 1958, pre-dating the Class 121s. Used on branch lines and for strengthening other services, this fleet did not last long as the lines they were built for started to be closed shortly after their construction. However, many found use as departmental units and some of the survivors found their way into operation on West Country branches. Some of the units lasted long enough to survive into preservation.

Chapter 1
Scotrail Survivors

In 1994, there were two distinct groups of DMU operating in Scotland. A small fleet of Class 101 units based at Corkerhill, Glasgow, which worked around all services on a few local routes, and a small fleet of Class 117 units based at Haymarket, Edinburgh, which operated peak-hour services on the Fife Circle (see below) and were valued for their people-shifting capabilities.

Fleet position as of April 1994:

Corkerhill

Set	DMBS	DMSL	Set	DMBS	DMSL
101684	51187	51509	101691	51253	53171
101686	51231	51500	101692	53253	53170
101687	51247	51512	101693	51192	53266
101688	51431	51501	101694	51188	53268
101689	51185	51511	101695	51226	51499
101690	51435	53177			

Haymarket

Set	DMBS	TSL	DMS	Set	DMBS	TSL	DMS
117301	51353	59505	51395	117311	51334	59500	51376
117306	51369	59521	51411	117313	51339	59492	51382
177308	51371	59509	51413	117314	51352	59489	51394
117310	51373	59486	51415				

Class 101s were all in Strathclyde orange livery, except 101692, which was in Caledonian Railway Blue. The whole 117 fleet was in Regional Railways livery.

The Paisley Canal line trains usually started from the far-flung corner of Glasgow Central, away from the hustle and bustle of the main station. This is where Class 101 set 101684 with DMBS 51187 leading awaits commencement of its journey on 13 September 1999.

After calling at Dunkeld, the line continues to Corkerhill, where Class 101 set 101694 with DMBS 51188 leading is calling on 28 April 1999. The line was electrified this far to give electric units access to Cockerhill depot; the headshunt for the depot is seen on the right.

Right: Class 101 set 101691 with DMSL 53171 leading approaches Mosspark on 26 May 1999. After Cockerhill, the line was double track for a short distance.

Below: Class 101 set 101691 with DMBS 51231 leading at the start of the single track to Paisley Canal, shortly before arriving at Crookston on 26 May 1999.

Class 101 set 101694 with DMBS 51188 trailing is seen leaving Hawkhead on 28 April 1999. The fencing and gate on the right of the photo is the boundary with the oil terminal (since closed), which was as far as freight worked following the 1983 closure to passengers.

Class 101 set 101694 arrives at Paisley Canal with DMBS 51188 leading on 10 April 2000. The condition of the track at this time left something to be desired. You can almost feel the 'bounce' in the sprung seat cushions.

Class 101 set 101684 at the end of the line at Paisley Canal on 26 May 1999. The original Paisley Canal station was on the other side of the bridge, behind the photographer. The line carried on a few miles more, but this section is now a cycle route. There was a basic service of two trains per hour operated by three units, although there were no trains on Sundays.

Trains to Whifflet

In 1993, the reopening of a Strathclyde route that had been closed since 1966 brought back into operation a train service from Glasgow to Whifflet. It was worked almost exclusively by Corkerhill Class 101 power twins until replaced by Class 156s in 2000. The line has been electrified since 2014.

Above: Having reached the end of its short journey from Glasgow Central, Class 101 set 101684 sits at Whifflet on a damp 8 March 2000.

Right: Class 101 set 101684 is seen through the waiting room window arriving at Bargeddie on 8 March 2000, shortly before the end of Class 101s on this route.

Class 101 set 101692 with DMSL 53170 trailing leaves Mount Vernon for Whifflet on 28 April 1999. This unit was repainted into pseudo–Caledonian Railway livery in 1996.

Caledonian Blue-liveried Class 101 set 101692 with DMBS 53253 leading under the roof of Glasgow Central, waiting departure for Whifflet on 24 May 1999. Both vehicles from this set have been preserved and can be seen at the Ecclesbourne Valley Railway but are no longer in their Caledonian Blue livery.

Motherwell to Cumbernauld

This is an important line for freight and was electrified to Coatbridge Central and Mossend for access to the yards near there and for passenger trains on the Argyle Line. In 1996, Strathclyde introduced an extension of this route along the unelectrified line to Cumbernauld. This operated hourly using one Class 101 unit running between Motherwell and Cumbernauld. All the Class 101s were replaced by Class 156s in 2000, and the line has since been electrified. Interestingly, 101692 was repainted into Caledonian Blue livery for the opening of this line and performed quite regularly on this service, although I never managed to photograph it on this line.

Right: Having reached Cumbernauld from Motherwell, Class 101 set 101695 waits to reverse and return to Motherwell on 2 February 1999.

Below: Working the shuttle between Motherwell and Cumbernauld, Class 101 set 101695 (51226 and 51499) is seen at Motherwell on 28 April 1999.

Class 101 set 101689 with DMSL 51511 leading pauses at the wet, dreary and seemingly deserted station of Greenfaulds on its way from Cumbernauld to Motherwell on 8 March 2000.

Probably more famous in enthusiast circles for its marshalling yards, which are the biggest in Scotland, Class 101 set 101695 pulls into Coatbridge Central on 28 April 1999.

Another route out of Glasgow that saw Heritage DMU operation was the Glasgow and South Western route. The Heritage operation of this route consisted of a few peak hour services from Glasgow Central to Barrhead supplementing the main service to Kilmarnock and Dumfries. Caledonian Blue Class 101 set 101692 briefly halts at the intriguingly named Crossmyloof on 25 May 1999.

Local stopping services from Glasgow Central to Barrhead were normally operated by a single Class 101 diagram interspersed with one Class 156, as demonstrated by Class 101 set 101691 sitting in the bay at Barrhead on 13 September 1999.

The Fife Circle

The Fife Circle serves towns to the north and east of Edinburgh and carries heavy commuter traffic. Extra trains were required in peaks, and thanks to their ability to hold lots of passengers, combined with the lack of newer trains that could be spared, six three-car Class 117 sets were transferred north to Haymarket from the Western Region in 1992. This service took Heritage DMUs over the iconic Forth Bridge. They kept going until withdrawal in 1999. The busyness of the Fife peak services has continued to cause headaches, and for a while locomotive-hauled trains were used until enough 'modern' DMUs became spare as a result of electrification schemes. There are now finally concrete plans to electrify this important service.

Left: Meetings in Haymarket train maintenance depot (TMD) sometimes went on quite late, as demonstrated by the position of the sun on Class 117 set 117308 at Haymarket on 17 July 1996.

Below: This is the view that would meet you as you walked down the access road to the depot from the station, with the Murrayfield Stadium as a backdrop. Class 117 sets 117308 and 117306 rest between peaks at Haymarket TMD on 29 April 1999.

Scotrail Survivors

Leaving Edinburgh Waverley and about to enter Mound Tunnels (above which this photo was taken) is Class 117 set 117313 on 17 July 1996.

Class 117 set 117310 awaits departure from Edinburgh Waverley with a Fife Circle train on 18 November 1995.

Above: Class 117 set 117306 leaves Edinburgh Waverley on 17 July 1996. Fife Circle trains usually left from bay platforms on the north side of Waverley station.

Left: Knowing that time for these operations was now limited, I opted to take a trip around the Fife Circle on a DMU. Class 117 set 117313 has just arrived at Cowdenbeath on 29 April 1999.

Class 117 set 117301 with DMS 51395 leading at North Queensferry on 29 April 1999. This is the first station north of the Forth Bridge. It was quite an experience travelling over the massive iconic bridge in a little DMU.

Chapter 2

The Far West to St Ives

Most Heritage DMU operations were in and around cities, but one of the more scenic locations in which they worked was the West Country. The South Wales and West franchise inherited a residual operation of four Heritage DMUs based at Penzance and working the St Erth to St Ives branch, unfortunately, however, it was also the first of the train operators to lose its Heritage units. These DMUs were always problematic, and the franchise substituted them with spare Class 153s whenever available. The two three-car units lost their trailer cars in 1995, and the end came in 1997, when the last unit, 101842, was withdrawn. The units were all in Network South East livery except set 117305, which retained its special GWR '150' chocolate and cream livery until the end.

Fleet position in April 1994:

Set	DMBS	TS	DMCL
101842	53314	59110	53327

Set	DMBS	TSL	DMS	Set	DMBS	DMS
117305	51368	59520	51410	117709	51344	51366
117708	51336	59520	51378			

Class 117 set 117708 leaving St Erth for St Ives on 4 August 1995. This was one of the few trains at that time that used the bay platform at St Erth, as most of the services ran to and from Penzance.

This was a grab shot of Class 101 set 101842 DMCL 53327 at St Erth on 12 July 1996 – this also turned out to be my last photo of a DMU operating in Cornwall on the main line. We were coming back from our holiday in the adjacent HST when I caught this through the window.

What makes this short line as stunning as it is are the views, which on a sunny summer's day are second to none. Class 117 set 117708 with DMBS 51336 leading slows for the stop at Carbis Bay on its way from St Erth to St Ives on 4 August 1995.

On the rear of the train above was Class 101 set 101842. It was quite normal for trains to be formed of two units in the summer, as a Park & Ride station at Lelant Saltings provided a healthy number of passengers seeking an alternative to parking in St Ives.

Class 117 set 117708 DMS 51378 at Penzance on 4 August 1995. The train is now berthed after working the last train of the day into Penzance. A nice touch is the welcome sign made out of local granite and inscribed with the Cornish language.

Above: Class 101 set 101842, with DMCL 53327 at the other end of the train, at Penzance on 4 August 1995.

Left: Class 117 DMBS 51362 is in Long Rock TMD at Penzance on 4 August 1995. This was part of Class 117 set 117021, which was sent down from London to help with the reliability issues.

Below: Class 117 DMBS 51344 at Long Rock TMD on 28 April 1995. Units could often be found stored here out of service. Unfortunately, this vehicle did not make it into preservation.

Class 119 set 119021 at Long Rock TMD on 4 August 1995. This unit was extracted from the Tyseley Cross City pool (see Chapter 6) again to help with the reliability problems, but for various reasons was found to be unusable.

Right: You can almost hear the rasp of the exhaust as Class 117 set 101842 leaves an unusually quiet Penzance for St Ives on 14 September 1995. This is the southernmost station in Great Britain, although surprisingly not the westernmost – that privilege lies with Arisaig on the West Highland Line.

Below: The terminus at St. Ives is a shadow of what it was in Great Western Railway days, but at least it is still open. The line has been shortened a little, and nearly all of the railway land has been given over to car parking. Class 101 set 101842 finds a little space to call in and pick up passengers on 15 September 1995.

Chapter 3
North London Variety

In the early 1990s, a few residual Heritage workings remained around London. By April 1994, these had been concentrated at the Bletchley traction maintenance depot (TMD) and operated on three routes using a mix of two-car Class 117 units and single-car Class 121. The two lines in inner London, the West London line and the Gospel Oak to Barking line, were eventually both electrified and now form part of the London Overground network having changed out of all recognition. The Bletchley to Bedford line, known as the 'Marston Vale line', has had a much more troubled life and just about hangs on, although it should eventually form part of the East West line between Oxford and Cambridge.

The units allocated to Bletchley TMD in April 1994 were as follows:

Class 117*

Set	DMBS	DMS	Set	DMBS	DMS
117700	51332	51374	117706	51366	51408
117701	51350	51392	117707	51335	51377
117702	51356	51398	117720	51364	51396
117703	51359	51401	117721	51363	51405
117704	51341	51383	117722	51345	51387
117705	51358	51400			

* Although the Bletchley Class 117 units were allocated set numbers in the 117 range, many carried the old set number prefixed by 'L' for 'London'. For example, 117707 carried the set number L707.

Class 121

Set	DMBS	Set	DMBS
121023	55023	121029	55029
121027	55027	121031	55031

Both the Class 117 and 121 units came from the Western Region, having previously been based at Reading and Old Oak Common and used on Thames Valley services out of Paddington, together with the related branches. The Class 117 sets were originally three-car, but the centre trailer car was removed before transfer to the North London operation.

When the franchise commenced operation, it was known as North London Railways but later on and just before the Heritage units were withdrawn it assumed the name of Silverlink. All of the Heritage DMU vehicles used by North London were painted in Network South East colours except one Class 121 vehicle, which was painted green, and another which acquired Silverlink colours near the end.

The West London line

The West London line last had through local passenger services up to the onset of World War Two. A couple of rush-hour trains operated to Kensington Olympia from Clapham Junction in the 1940s, and in the 1980s cross-country Inter City trains to and from the South Coast commenced. The route remained heavily used for freight throughout the war.

North London Variety

The reintroduction of local passenger trains on the West London line started in May 1994 with a diesel service running from Clapham Junction to Willesden Junction, using two units and running every 30 minutes. At this time, there was only the one intermediate station, which was at Kensington Olympia. The service was known colloquially as the 'Willy Belle'. Electrification came in 1997 and, along with it, operation by Class 313 electric multiple units (EMUs). This was followed by the opening of more intermediate stations, and the line now forms part of the London Overground network.

Class 117 set L700 is seen at Willesden Junction with DMS 51374 leading on 30 November 1994, ready to return to Clapham Junction. The West London trains terminated in the high-level platform.

A very rare sight at Willesden Junction as Class 121 'Bubble Car' 55029 has arrived from Clapham Junction and has now set off to shunt for its return on 12 October 1995. This was so rare an occurence, that a friendly person at Bletchley depot who informed me early in the morning, giving me time to get this shot.

Occasionally, a spare unit could be found stabled in the bay platform of the low-level station, as demonstrated by Class 117 set L703 at Willesden Junction on 24 November 1994.

After a unit arrived at Willesden Junction and was emptied of passengers, it would then set off in the direction of Kensal Rise to crossover and come back along the track on the right to return to Clapham Junction. Class 117 set L703 performs this manoeuvre on 17 May 1995.

Class 117 set L707 shunts back to Willesden Junction on 30 November 1994. Note the old water tank in the background. There have been many changes in this area since this time, the major one being the replacement of the third rail. This route is now part of the London Overground network with a frequency of service and passenger level that would have been unthinkable in 1994!

Class 117 set L700 with DMBS 51332 leading at Kensington Olympia, the only intermediate station at the time, on 20 November 1994.

Class 117 set L707 at Kensington Olympia on 30 November 1994. This station has seen a mixed history of usage. Before the DMUs came, it was served by a couple of trains per day from Clapham Junction. There were also the now long-gone Motorail trains, and starting in the 1980s a number of Inter City trains from the north to the south coast ran on this route. These have also since ceased, leaving just the very frequent local service.

Class 117 set L702 is heading north to Willesden Junction at the site of the future station at Shepherd's Bush on 28 April 1995. I have strong family connections with this area and childhood memories of watching freight trains on the West London line. The construction of the massive Westfield Shopping Centre behind the photographer transformed the fortunes of Shepherd's Bush and had a very positive effect on the West London line.

On a very foggy 23 December 1994, Class 117 set L702 with DMBS 51356 leading sits in Platform 2 at Clapham Junction.

Class 117 set 117706 arrives at Clapham Junction on 5 May 1995. The skyline here has changed out of recognition. Where the chimneys of Battersea Power Station dominated, there are now the massive skyscrapers of the Nine Elms' development.

Class 117 set L707 at Clapham Junction on 13 October 1996. This is another scene that has changed thanks to London Overground. The unelectrified centre road is now electrified and is used as access to a new platform for trains on the South London line. The frequency of both routes is such that there always seems to be something moving.

For a couple of weeks in the summer of 1996, the electric service was suspended between Willesden Junction and Gunnersbury for electrification works and a substitute service operated by a couple of Class 117s was put in place. Class 117 set 117704 is at Willesden Junction on 7 September 1996, displaying its Richmond destination even though it is only going as far as Gunnersbury.

This substitution allowed a number of photos to be taken on a route that normally did not see these units. Here, Class 117 set 117704 crosses the Grand Union Canal near Willesden Junction on 7 September 1996.

In those distant pre-internet days, enthusiasts relied on contacts in train operating companies for information about less usual services and vehicles known to be passing along tracks. Class 117 set 117704 arrives at Willesden Junction off of the Richmond line on 7 September 1996. The usual West London line goes off to the left.

Above: Class 117 set 117704 arriving at Gunnersbury on 7 September 1996. The route has now been joined by the District Line Richmond branch, which explains the fourth rail in the track. The train is reversing as passengers from here to Richmond were expected to use the Underground.

Right: Class 117 set L705 with DMBS 51358 leading arrives at South Acton on 10 September 1996. Another area dear to me, as I went to school not far from here and ended my railway career at the nearby Acton Works.

Class 117 set L700 at Acton Central on 31 August 1996. The overhead wires are already up and are being commissioned. This is now the change point for the third rail.

The Gospel Oak to Barking line (the 'Goblin')

The Gospel Oak to Barking line is an intriguing railway that runs across North and East London, starting in the bay platform at Gospel Oak on the North London line and ending, at the time, in Barking. An urban backwater, it is amazing that the line managed to survive so long as it gave an air of advanced dereliction and decay and served very few interchanges. The line had been served by a variety of DMUs over the years, and finally, post-April 1994, by Class 117s based at Bletchley. The basic service was every 30 minutes and required three sets to operate the service. Although there were small pockets of electrification where other routes joined and left, the line was mostly diesel-operated. There was a busy freight business primarily from Tilbury to Willesden and onwards. Towards the end of 1999, the Class 117s were gradually replaced with Class 150/1 DMUs as they became available at Bletchley. The Class 150s were replaced by Class 172 DMUs when the route became part of the London Overground network and was electrified. It now thrives as a busy part of the London rail network and has even been extended at the eastern end to Barking Riverside. It is often referred to as the 'Goblin'.

Left: Class 117 set 117704 has arrived at Gospel Oak and terminated in the bay platform on 30 November 1994. The name 'Gospel Oak' was derived from a tree on the edge of Hampstead Heath, under which itinerant preachers used to preach the Gospel.

Below: Class 117 set L707 (117707) has arrived at Gospel Oak in the evening of 16 September 1999. It has disgorged its passengers, most of whom have probably found their way to the North London line platforms. The barking train sits in a bay, with the freight lines to the right connecting with the North London line behind the unit.

The quality of the track leaves a little bit to be desired as Class 117 set L703 bounces along at 20mph near Gospel Oak on 30 November 1994. All has changed here now. You would now need to be very tall to see over the bridge parapet, and even then the view would be blocked by overhead electrification.

Very rarely seen on this route but operating as a regulation pair, Class 121 55029 arrives at Upper Holloway on 13 August 1999. This was just before the arrival of Class 150 units gave some welcome relief.

The rear of the previous photo shows Class 121 55031 at Upper Holloway on 13 August 1999. Next to Upper Holloway station in Pemberton Gardens is the entrance to one of the last former tram depots in London, which is still in use as a bus garage. This image was taken after the ban on Class 121s operating singly so whenever they were out and about they operated in pairs.

Class 117 set L702 at Upper Holloway on a train heading for Barking on 13 August 1999. Passenger use was brisk but light, as there are a number of tube possibilities in the area. However, the spread of London's commercial areas eastwards has seen a bit of a resurgence in these once secondary routes.

Class 117 set L703 at Upper Holloway on 30 November 1994.

Famous for being a leafy and expensive part of North London, the station at Crouch Hill shows some signs of modernisation and upgrading to match its surroundings as Class 117 set L701 (117701) arrives on a Barking service on 27 August 1998. It is doubtful that many of the locals know of its existence, as there are a number of tube stations within walking distance.

Class 117 set L703 (117703) at Crouch Hill on a foggy 23 December 1994. For those interested in industrial archaeology, there is a former dairy a short walk from this station that has a number of restored terracotta frescoes in its wall.

Left: Seen from high up on a bridge on the former Great Northern Railway route from Finsbury Park to Highgate, Class 117 set L720 is seen through the undergrowth approaching Crouch Hill on 23 August 1999. In the distance, by the signal box, the junction for the spur to the East Coast Main Line, which passes over just beyond the arched bridge, can be seen.

Below: Class 117 set L702 with DMBS 51356 leading at Harringay Green Lanes on 10 May 1994. Privatisation had no effect on the livery of Class 117s, and they retained their Network South East colours until withdrawn, which was, to be fair, a little later than intended.

Class 117 set L701 at Harringay Green Lanes on 31 August 1999. This station was originally known as Harringay Stadium, but when the adjacent Greyhound Stadium closed it was renamed to reflect the culturally diverse and popular Green Lanes, which it passes over just behind the photographer.

Right: South Tottenham projects an air of importance far beyond what it should have. The overhead wires give a false impression of electrification, despite the core services still being diesel. Junctions at each end of the station allow trains to run from the Lea Valley route to Seven Sisters, and the wires were put up to facilitate this. All were controlled by the signal box seen here. Class 117 set L703 runs through this infrastructure on 30 November 1994.

Below: Class 117 set L703 arrives back at South Tottenham on 30 November 1994. The bridge in the background is part of the Seven Sisters line.

Class 117 set 117706 with DMS 51408 arrives at Blackhorse Road with a Barking train on 15 May 1995.

Blackhorse Road, which can be seen from the sign on the left is, aside from the major interchange of Barking, the only connection with the London Underground on the route. It is on the Victoria Line, which opened here in 1968, although it was not until 1981 that the Goblin station was re-sited to give better interchange served by a common booking office. Class 117 set L720 (117720) leaves Blackhorse Road with a Gospel Oak train on 23 August 1999.

Class 117 set L701 near Walthamstow Queen's Road on 26 January 1999, exhibiting the general run-down condition of the line and indeed the surrounding area at this time.

Class 117 set 117706 at Walthamstow Queen's Road on 26 January 1999. Although not touted as an interchange, those in the know would be able to find Walthamstow Central Underground and mainline station just a few minutes' walk away. This was typical of most of the stations on this route, which seemed to be hidden from public view, on a service that appeared to go from nowhere to nowhere. However, thanks to London Underground and decent advertising, it forms a useful route across North East London.

Class 117 set L704 runs into Leyton Midland Road on 15 October 1998. Midland Road is a reflection back to the joint ownership of the line by the Great Eastern Railway and the Midland Railway.

Class 117 set L700 comes to a halt at Leytonstone High Road on 10 October 1995. The burnt-out station building and lack of potential passengers was typical of this line at the time, a far cry from the bustling picture portrayed by today's Overground scene.

Out on the rooftops of London! Between Leyton and Wanstead Park, the line runs on a viaduct, as demonstrated here by Class 117 set L701 arriving at Leytonstone High Road on 12 March 1999.

Class 117 set L701 arriving at Leytonstone High Road on 12 March 1999. At this time, it was common for depots to embellish some of their older stock – note the red buffer beam and white rimmed buffers.

Still high up on its viaduct, Class 117 set L707 comes to a halt at a deserted Wanstead Park on 7 February 1995.

Class 117 set L720 at Woodgrange Park with a Barking train on 23 August 1999. The leading coach, DMS 51396, was unusual in that it did not have a headcode box. This came about following accident damage that required grafting a cab from a withdrawn Class 116 coach in 1987. The overhead wires here form a link between the Great Eastern Main Line and the London Tilbury and Southend line. The junction of the connecting spur can be seen under the bridge.

Barking is the end of the Goblin and is one of London's major transport interchanges. It is served by the District Line and C2C services to Southend and Shoeburyness, and until 2021 Gospel Oak trains terminated at this somewhat dingy platform. Class 117 set L707 is at Barking in October 1995.

The Marston Vale line

This is a remnant of the once fabled 'Varsity' line from Oxford to Cambridge and survived on the back of the large amount of school traffic it carries from isolated communities. It is no surprise that as a diesel line in a sea of electrification it was one of the last bastions of Heritage DMUs. Home to Bletchley TMD's Class 121 'Bubble Car' units, these operated singly on an hourly service with a Class 117 strengthening the school train. An incident in 1996 precluded the use of single Class 121s, and Class 117s took over the service, although the Class 121s could be operated in pairs. Eventually, at the end of the century, enough Class 150s and 153s became available and the DMUs faded into oblivion.

Right: Class 121 55023 is seen at Bletchley on 8 August 1994, having just arrived from Bedford. This unit was the last of its type to be given an overhaul and was painted in an approximation of its original green livery to mark the occasion.

Below: Class 121 55023, again at Bletchley, this time coupled to a Class 117 to work the school train on a cold and snowy 29 March 1995.

Class 117 set L721 (117721) leaves Bletchley on 14 April 1999 and passing Bletchley TMD heads for Bedford. The electrification seen here only goes a short distance and forms the access to the depot.

Class 121 55029 is picking up the odd passenger at Fenny Stratford on 8 September 1995. The line is double tracked for most of its length except a short singled section through this station, which is set in the suburbs of the city of Milton Keynes. This unit was adorned with white cab ends.

Class 117 set L702 is seen arriving at Bow Brickhill on 15 October 1998. At this time, this station was unique on this line in having staggered platforms to try and avoid traffic congestion at the level crossing. Despite being within the urban Milton Keynes area, usage is very light.

Class 121 55029 has paused at Woburn Sands with a Bedford train on 26 November 1994.

Above: Class 117 set L704 with DMBS 51341 leading arrives at Woburn Sands with a Bletchley train on 17 February 1999. At this time, semaphore signals still existed and can be glimpsed in the background behind the unit.

Left: Class 117 set L701 leaves Ridgmont on 16 April 1999 and heads for Bedford. Note the level crossing gates of the traditional type; these were controlled from a small frame in part of the station building.

Class 121 55029 at Ridgmont on 26 November 1994. The Bubble Car is heading for Bletchley with the gates already closed behind it. The country station atmosphere is spoilt a little by the Network South East paraphernalia, and a lot more by the noise from the M1 motorway nearby.

Above: Class 121 55023 in the heart of the Bedfordshire Brickworks at Kempston Hardwick on 26 November 1994. Although a tiny and basic halt, to the left of the picture was a massive brickworks whose chimneys could be seen for miles around. Sadly, all is now gone.

Right: Class 121 55031 at the 'new' Bedford St Johns on 29 March 1995. Until 1984, the trains terminated in the old Bedford St Johns station. Common sense prevailed, however, and the line was diverted to terminate in the far busier Bedford Midland station giving a far greater range of connections. A new platform at St Johns was constructed on the connecting spur.

Class 121 55029 at Bedford Midland on 13 February 1995. This is the school train, which was strengthened with a Class 117 set on the rear.

Loans and off the beaten track

Class 117 set L701 at Watford Junction in May 1999. It is berthed following its use on the St Albans Abbey branch the previous weekend, whilst attention was being paid to the overhead electrification.

For a short period of time, First Great Eastern were without any DMUs to operate the Sudbury branch line. As they could not be used singly at the time on the Marston Vale line, a Class 121 was loaned to operate on the branch. Class 121 55029 is seen at Marks Tey awaiting departure to Sudbury on 31 December 1997.

Class 121 55029 after arrival at the rather basic terminus of Sudbury from Marks Tey on 31 December 1997. In the background, the leisure centre that covers much of the site of the original Great Eastern Railway station can be seen. Whilst operating the branch, the Class 121s received appropriate route branding stickers featuring the viaduct at Chappel & Wakes Colne, the home of the East Anglian Railway Museum.

Class 121 55023 at Chalfont & Latimer in March 2000. This unit has probably had the happiest time in preservation of the Bletchley Bubbles. This went straight from operation to preservation at the Chinnor & Princes Risborough Railway, where it remains to this day. Whilst at the time of this photo the unit was in preservation, it had retained its mainline certificate and is working on the 'mainline' (albeit the London Underground) and has therefore been included.

Bletchley TMD

As mentioned earlier, the North London fleet was maintained at Bletchley TMD, which, as time went on, became a collection point for various Heritage vehicles in various states of disrepair. The following photos give an idea of what could be found in the latter years of the Heritage DMUs.

Class 117 DMS 51400 was a spare coach at Bletchley TMD on 3 February 2000. This vehicle has been preserved and currently is stored at the Wensleydale Railway.

Class 117 DMBS 51368 at Bletchley TMD on 14 April 1999. Unfortunately, despite its celebrity status of being part of the Great Western-liveried set, 117305 didn't make it into preservation. Instead, it ended up moving from Bletchley to Penzance to provide spares.

Class 121 55027 in company with a Class 117 in Bletchley stabling sidings in August 1994. This was on the official (long) walking route from the station to the depot.

Class 121 55031 at Bletchley TMD on 3 February 2000. From here, it had an interesting future, becoming part of the Network Rail Severn Tunnel rescue train for which it was heavily modified. It then became a spares donor to keep Arriva Wales 55032 running and eventually found its way to the Ecclesbourne Valley Railway, where it is to be used as a store – preservation of sorts!

Nameplate as fitted to Class 121 55031. It was very rare for DMUs to be named, but the following names were carried by Class 121s:

121027 *Bletchley T.M.D.*   Named to commemorate the depot.
121029 *Marston Vale*   Named to represent the area around the Bletchley to Bedford line.
121031 *Leslie Crabbe*   Named after a railwayman who tirelessly campaigned to support the Marston Vale Line.

Class 121 55027 at Bletchley TMD on 3 February 2000. This unit was the only one at Bletchley to be repainted into Silverlink colours. This vehicle is currently preserved at the Ecclesbourne Valley Railway, and as time and resources become available it will be restored as a vehicle to assist the Permanent Way department.

Class 121 55029 at Bletchley TMD on 14 April 1999. After passenger use finished, this vehicle became a camera train for Euroscout GB. After becoming surplus to requirements in 2010, it was purchased by the Rushden Transport Museum, but restoration has been slow.

Right: Class 117 set L704 with DMBS 51314 leading is at the back of Bletchley TMD on 16 May 1995 with a withdrawn Class 310 electric multiple unit (EMU) behind. 51341 was preserved but only to act as part of a scheme by Dorset County Council to reopen the Swanage Railway into Wareham. When this fell through, the vehicle was stripped for spares and eventually scrapped at the Dean Forest Railway.

Below: Class 117 set 117706 at Bedford rounds off this section of the Bletchley-based North London Heritage DMU units on 23 January 1999.

Chapter 4
Manchester's Mechanicals

At the time of privatisation, by far the biggest fleet of Heritage DMUs by size and geographical spread in operation. The entire fleet was based at Longsite TMD in Manchester. Operationally, they could be seen over a fair amount of the North West and North Wales. From March 1997, the services were operated by First North Western, part of the First Group, and this was the case until the final units ran in 2003. This was the last area to operate Heritage units on any scale, bar the last few Class 121 units later operated by Arriva Wales and Chiltern Railways.

All of the units operated in this area were Class 101s built by Metropolitan Cammell. Most retained their Regional Railways livery to the end, although one unit, 101683, was repainted green and unsurprisingly given the nickname of 'Daisy' after the DMU featured in the *Thomas the Tank Engine* books. Unit 101840 also retained its Network South East livery until withdrawal. Most of the sets were two cars, as the two three-car units lost their centre cars. The sets were a mix of power twin units and those with a single power car and a driving trailer.

Towards the very end, after 2000, the fleet was enhanced by the arrival of ex-Corkerhill power twins from Scotland. Following this, a large amount of random reformation was undertaken just to keep things running, including the introduction of three-car power sets. A large number of vehicles entered preservation, but these have since been reduced as the preservation world realised the effort required to keep these machines operable.

Fleet position as of April 1994:

Set	DMBS	DTSL	Set	DMBS	DTSL
101651	53201	54379	101659	51213	54352
101652	53198	54346	101660	51189	54343
101653	51426	54358	101661	51463	54365
101654	51800	54408	101662	53228	54055
101655	51428	54062	101663	51201	54347
101656	51230	54056	101664	51442	54061
101657	53211	54085	101665	51429	54393
101658	51175	54091			

Set	DMBS	DMSL	Set	DMBS	DMSL
101676	51205	51803	101681	51228	51506
101677	51179	51496	101682	53256	51505
101678	51210	53746	101835	51432	51498
101679	51224	51533	101840	53311	53322
101680	53204	53163	101841	53312	53332

Set	DMBS	TCL	DMSL
101683	51177	59303	53629
101685	53164	59539	53160

South Manchester

In 1994, Manchester Piccadilly was very much a centre of Heritage DMU operations, together with the infamous Class 142 'Pacer' units and a myriad of electric traction and more modern DMUs. Most of the operations were to the south and east of Manchester, mostly in the suburbs but with some workings along the Hope Valley line on stopping services to Sheffield. This was a complicated route network in which a number of lines were intertwined. These routes proved to be the last intensely operated Heritage DMU services, with some hanging on until the end in 2003, although by then many diagrams had been replaced. The routes covered were:

Manchester Piccadilly–Guide Bridge–Romiley–Rose Hill Marple
Manchester Piccadilly–Romiley–New Mills Central–Sheffield
Manchester Piccadilly–Stockport
Stockport–Stalybridge (restricted service)

The Rose Hill service was hourly, and the Hope Valley line service was half-hourly to Marple, hourly to New Mills and a two-hourly stopping service to Sheffield. The Stockport to Stalybridge service ran once per week and was effectively a parliamentary service run to avoid a closure process. This route is still in service to this day.

The journey to Rose Hill commences at Manchester Piccadilly, where Class 101 set 101665 arrives from Rose Hill on 24 March 1999. This is Manchester's main station, with others located at Manchester Victoria and Manchester Oxford Road.

Class 101 set 101653 passes Ardwick on 8 May 2000. Ardwick was the first station from Manchester Piccadilly on the Great Central Main Line via Woodhead but had very few trains stopping there, only in the peaks at this time and none of them DMUs.

In a location looking a little run-down, Class 101 set 101661 with DTSL 54365 leading approaches Gorton on 28 February 1995 on a Rose Hill via Guide Bridge service. This Manchester suburb used to be home to the Gorton Works of the Great Central Railway and the works of Beyer, Peacock & Co, making it a centre of railway industry. All of this, together with much other industry, has sadly long gone. 54365 unfortunately went the same way as much of its surroundings, being sold as a source of spare parts for other preserved vehicles and having since been scrapped.

Class 101 set 101657 with DMBS 53211 leading at Guide Bridge on 28 February 1995. This station was once a major junction on the Great Central Railway Woodhead route to Sheffield with fast electric-hauled Manchester to Sheffield expresses passing through. By the time this photo was taken, the Woodhead route was long gone, and the only trains were very few freights and trains to Rose Hill and Hadfield, together with the very infrequent service from Stalybridge to Stockport line passed through. There has been a resurgence as the route from Stalybridge is now used by a number of TransPennine trains into Manchester Piccadilly.

Having left the electrified remainder of the former Great Central Woodhead route to Hadfield, Class 101 set 101657 is now on the secondary route to Romiley and is calling at the first station, North Hyde, on 12 April 2000.

Moving from the previous photo, Class 101 set 101661 is seen calling at Hyde Central on 12 April 2000. Hyde is a suburb of Greater Manchester, but the rather basic nature of both Hyde stations is testament to their relatively light usage. Hyde is served by a number of stations and bus routes, making the hourly service on offer at this time not so attractive.

Just coming to a halt, Class 101 set 101661 with DTSL 54365 is seen at the attractive and leafy station of Woodley on 12 November 1999. The set of points in the foreground allow refuse trains to cross over to reach the spur to the Bredbury refuse processing plant.

Class 101 set 101685 comes to a halt at Romiley on 3 March 1999. This town used to host the well-known railway brake manufacturer Davies and Metcalfe. The factory is long gone, but the name lives on in the railway supply industry.

Right: Class 101 set 101653 approaching Rose Hill on 12 November 1999. This is a short single-track spur from the route through Bredbury to New Mills and Chinley, leaving this line a short distance after Romiley. At this time, nearly all services on this line were in the hands of Class 101s, with just the occasional substitution by Class 142 Pacer units.

Below: Class 101 set 101653 at Rose Hill on 12 November 1999. The route once carried on to Macclesfield beyond the buffer stop in the background, but this closed in January 1970. It is now part of a walking and cycling route called the Middlewood Way.

Power twin Class 101 set 101678 with DMBS 51210 at Manchester Piccadilly on 12 November 1999. Until the end of the DMUs in 2003, it was very unusual not to see a Heritage unit in one of platforms 1, 2 or 3 idling away the time before its next working.

Class 101 set 101658 passes through Ardwick on 8 May 2000 on a service to Marple via Romiley. The tracks on the left are the main line to Stockport and the South. The unit is taking the former Great Central Railway route that once formed the famous Woodhead route to Sheffield.

Class 101 set 101661 passes through Ashburys with a train to Marple on 12 April 2000. This station is actually in the suburb of Openshaw, and the name referred to the Ashbury Carriage and Wagon Company, which was located nearby but has now long gone.

Ryder Brow station is relatively new, having been opened in 1985 by British Rail as a Greater Manchester initiative. Unfortunately, it is relatively lightly used. Class 101 set 101660 has just arrived at Ryder Brow from Marple on 12 February 2000.

101654 is arriving at Romiley on 12 February 2000 with a service to Marple. Romiley is a suburban hub as there are junctions at each end of the station, to the west for Manchester via Bredbury and Guide Bridge, and to the east towards Rose Hill and the Hope Valley route.

Class 101 set 101678 on a stopping train to Sheffield via the Hope Valley line at Bredbury on 12 November 1999. These trains were and still are very popular with walkers heading for the Pennines at weekends. I have experienced the crush in a Pacer travelling to Edale for just that reason.

Class 101 set 101681 has arrived at Bredbury with a train from New Mills Central on 12 November 1999.

Class 101 set 101665 shunts at Marple on 7 January 1995. The unit has just arrived and terminated on a train from Manchester and is making the shunt move to return from whence it came. The track condition demonstrates the secondary nature of this route, with mainline trains between Manchester and Sheffield diverted via Stockport and the Hazel Grove spur.

After their usage in Scotland had finished, most of the surviving Glasgow Class 101s were transferred south to Manchester to help out their Longsite cousins. Their short-term life expectancy meant that the livery was never amended. Class 101 set 101695 is seen on a Hope Valley service to Sheffield at Marple in February 2001.

To aid with reliability, which by this time was ailing, most of the driving trailer sets were split up and the power cars were randomly placed with power twins to make up what was effectively 'power triples'. Here, power car 51230 from set 101656 runs into Marple with a train for New Mills Central on 20 February 2001.

Class 101 set 101681 at New Mills Central on 29 August 1998. The unit has arrived and terminated, and after depositing its passengers it is now retracing its steps to the stabling siding where it will wait time before returning to Manchester. New Mills is an attractive town set in a steep valley with lots of industrial heritage harking back to its days as a mill town.

Class 101 set 101661 is working a Manchester Piccadilly to Sheffield Hope Valley stopping service and has arrived at New Mills Central on 29 August 1998. 101681 from the previous photo can be glimpsed in the siding behind the rear carriage.

Departing Chinley for its trip over the Hope Valley line as a stopping train, green Class 101 set 101685 is seen on 4 February 2001. From here to Sheffield is one of the most scenic railway routes in Britain, passing through the heart of the Pennines. As well as providing an essential local service, the stopping trains are very heavily loaded with walkers at the weekend.

Class 101 set 101676 gets ready to leave for Manchester from Sheffield on 4 February 1999. This was the usual bay platform at Sheffield for the stopping trains to Manchester via the Hope Valley line, with departures roughly every two hours.

On a cold 28 February 1995, Class 101 set 101681 is seen at Stockport on a Hazel Grove to Manchester Piccadilly working. Assuming the heaters are operational in the unit, those with such memories can almost feel the welcoming 'fug' inside.

Class 101 set 101685 is at Stockport, having just worked from Manchester Piccadilly on 8 May 2000. After a peak-hour run to Hazel Grove and back to Stockport, it will be shunted into the sidings. Both vehicles of this set were preserved at the North Yorkshire Moors Railway.

After the morning peak, and in the reverse direction for the evening peak, there were several empty stock workings to and from the carriage sidings behind Stockport station. Class 101 set 101653 arrives at Stockport from Manchester Piccadilly on one such working on 28 February 1995.

Another ex-Scotrail Class 101 unit, 101693, is arriving at Manchester Piccadilly in February 2001. It will be noted that absolutely no attempt has been made to replace any of the Strathclyde and Scotrail branding, something that would probably not be tolerated nowadays!

Gogledd Cymru a Dyffryn Conwy/North Wales and the Conwy Valley

Class 101s have had quite a long association with North Wales, and this lasted almost to the end of DMU operation, with gradual substitution of newer units as and when they became available. The routes covered were:

   Chester–Llandudno Junction–Holyhead
   Llandudno–Llandudno Junction–Bleanau Ffestiniog (Conwy Valley line)
   Bidston–Shotton–Wrexham Central

The first route saw occasional stopping services worked by Class 101s; the Conwy Valley line was usually the complete service; and there was one diagram on the Wrexham line usually shared with a Class 153 or 156 unit.

Right: Still running as a three-car unit at this time, Class 101 set 101685 was often allocated to a diagram that took it from Chester to Holyhead, back to Llandudno Junction then back to Holyhead and on to Chester. After a very early start, I picked it up at Chester, where it is seen on a very wet 10 February 1995.

Below: Having taken a trip down the Conwy Valley and back on a Class 150, I next caught up with Class 101 set 101685 at Llandudno Junction, where it sits in the bay platform waiting its return to Holyhead on 10 February 1995. Not long after this, it lost its centre car, 59539, which went for storage at Blackpool North and since has entered preservation.

Class 101 set 101678 sits in the bay platform at Llandudno Junction on 25 August 1995 waiting to form a stopping service to Holyhead.

Left: Sitting in the sunshine, 101676 awaits departure for Blaenau Ffestiniog at Llandudno on 26 April 2000. In a useful nod to connectivity, most Conwy Valley trains run to and from Llandudno, which is a major seaside resort. This allows people to take a day trip along the Conwy Valley without having to change trains.

Below: On a more, perhaps typical, dull summer's day, Class 101 set 101679 with DMSL 51533 leading is at Llandudno ready to work down the Conwy Valley on 25 August 1995.

Later that day, the sun came out and illuminated Class 101 set 101679 with DMBS 51224 trailing at Llandudno Junction, on 25 August 1995. This is a mid-day service that terminated at Llandudno Junction and quickly returned to Blaenau Ffestiniog.

Staff converse at Llandudno Junction before Class 101 set 101677 leaves on 12 January 2000 for Blaenau Ffestiniog. This mid-winter shot demonstrates quite clearly the seasonal traffic on the North Wales line as the station is almost deserted compared with the bustling summer months.

I managed to convince my family to have a week in Betws-y-Coed, making no secret that it may be the last time we would see Heritage DMU units on the Conwy Valley line. In weather seemingly typical for a Buck family holiday, the train we are about to catch to Blaenau Ffestiniog arrived with 101682 at Betws-y-Coed on 9 August 2000.

Later that day, we returned to Llanrwst with the intention of witnessing the token change at the signal box, which has just been performed as Class 101 set 101682 arrives at North Llanrwst on 9 August 2000.

Class 101 set 101676 leaves the impressive London and North Western Railway station at Betws-y-Coed on 26 April 2000. To the right are some of the tracks in the Betws-y-Coed railway museum. Betws was a resort town from the Victorian times and has a station building to match, although these days none of it is in use.

This was the last time I saw a Heritage DMU on the Conwy Valley line, and it was just by chance as we were making our way home. Roman Bridge is a splendid location in the heart of Snowdonia, and I was so glad that we stopped here. Class 101 set 101676 calls on its way to Blaenau Ffestiniog on 11 August 2000.

Class 101 set 101679 with DMSL 51533 nearest the camera has reached the end of the line at Blaenau Ffestiniog on 25 August 1995. Note the narrow-gauge line of the Ffestiniog Railway on the left. This station is on the site of the former Great Western Railway, and the line was extended to meet the Ffestiniog Railway in 1983.

Above: Yet again, Class 101 set 101679 is seen at Blaenau Ffestiniog, five years after the last photo, on 19 July 2000, this time with DMBS 51224 nearest the camera. Since that time, it appears that the Ffestiniog Railway has extended its loop line further around the platform. In the background, some of the slate waste that Blaenau is famous for can be seen.

Left: Class 101 set 101678 at Bidston on 14 March 2000. This station is actually on the Merseyrail network and offers connections into and out of Liverpool. Trains to and from Wrexham terminated here and after a quick turnaround took the route to the left in the background.

Class 101 set 101683 arriving at Shotton on 12 January 2001. This line continued on to Wrexham Central, and normally only one diagram out of the three on this route was operated by Class 101. Shotton also has low-level platforms on the North Wales Main Line.

North West

The North West is a catch-all phrase to describe the large number of local routes north and west of Manchester extending out to Macclesfield (which is in fact south west) Chester and Wigan. There were a number of routes where odd diagrams were operated by Class 101s interspersed with Class 142s and 150s and even 156s. In theory, a Class 101 could turn up anywhere if crew knowledge was available and there was a shortage of more modern units. However, the following are the more regular routes that they could be seen on:

Manchester Oxford Road–Irlam
Manchester Piccadilly–Altrincham–Sale–Chester
Manchester Piccadilly–Macclesfield
Manchester Victoria–Wigan Wallgate–Southport
Crewe–Chester

Right: Class 101 set 101662 with DTSL 54055 leading waits to leave Manchester Piccadilly with a stopping service to Macclesfield on 27 January 1995. Although this route is entirely electrified, the odd peak service was worked by a Class 101 owing to a shortage of EMUs.

Below: Class 101 set 101654 has arrived at Macclesfield in the evening of 8 May 2000. This was an unusual working in that it travelled entirely under the wires along the West Coast Main Line. It ran empty back to Longsite TMD.

Class 101 set 101654 at Manchester Oxford Road on 5 September 1995. This station is often overlooked but is very busy as it serves central Manchester. It was rebuilt in 1960 in a modernistic style using large quantities of wood. Now a listed building, it requires a lot of maintenance.

Left: When originally set up in 1968, Public Transport Executives (PTE) were keen to use their new powers to enhance transport in their areas. This often meant new services ending at border points of their territory when through services may have been more logical and efficient, although the progress was made at the time was good. On the edge of Greater Manchester is Irlam, where Class 101 set 101654 with DTSL 54408 leading waits patiently to return to Manchester Oxford Road on 5 September 1995.

Below: Class 101 set 101680 on an Irlam service at Manchester Oxford Road on 3 March 1999.

Class 101 set 101663 arrives at Deansgate with a train from Irlam on 10 December 1999. This has run along part of the Cheshire Lines Committee route from Liverpool to Manchester via Warrington. The viaduct in the background carries part of the Metrolink tram system.

Right: Class 101 set 101664 with DMBS 51442 nearest the camera stands spare in a bay platform at Chester on 11 March 1999. There were a number of Class 101-worked routes into Chester from Crewe, Manchester Piccadilly and the North Wales line.

Below: Class 101 set 101665 leaving Chester for Manchester Piccadilly on 11 March 1999. These trains took the ex-Cheshire Lines Committee route to Manchester via Knutsford and Altrincham.

Waiting to form a Manchester Piccadilly via Sale and Altrincham train, Class 101 set 101679 is seen at a very wet Chester on 20 October 1997.

Class 101 set 101681 at Chester Depot on 25 August 1995. It was quite often that a spare unit would be stabled on the site of what was the old Chester DMU depot. This is now the site of the Chester Alstom TMD, where the fleet of Class 175 Coradia DMUs is maintained.

Class 101 set 101665 at Manchester Oxford Road on 23 March 1999. I am not sure what this working is, but there is a reasonable chance that it is headed for Irlam, despite the destination saying Warrington Central. This would be possible if it was covering for the non-availability of more modern units.

Returning from Southport via Wigan, Class 101 set 101682 calls at Bolton on its way to Manchester Victoria on 5 September 1995. The scene here has changed drastically since the route to Preston and Blackpool was electrified.

Class 101 set 101682 with DMSL 51505 leading arrives at Wigan Wallgate on 5 September 1995, with a train from Southport to Manchester Victoria. The perils of slam-door stock are demonstrated here, as someone has already opened a door way before the train has come to a stop.

Class 101 set 101835 at Crewe on 8 October 1998, waiting to depart for Holyhead via Chester. These were the days before Chester had the volume of through trains from London that it has today. There were a number of connecting shuttles operating the short distance to Chester. This set had a unique livery, as Regional Railways' colours had been applied around the ex-Network South East livery. The London origin of the set is given away by the 'L' next to the set number.

An oddball in the North West fleet, Network South East-liveried Class 101 set 101840 is arriving at Manchester Oxford Road on a working to Chester on 23 March 1999. This station is architecturally quite unique.

Longsight TMD

All of the Manchester-based units were maintained at Longsight. This massive depot was operated by Alstom, pre-empting the soon-to-be-introduced Pendolino trains on the West Coast route. The First North Western units were, in theory, a guest, but as Longsight had maintained the DMUs for a very long time there was a large expertise amongst the staff and virtually any task could be accomplished.

Above: A number of Class 101 units including Network South East-liveried 101840 are stabled outside Longsite TMD on 9 August 1995.

Right: Class 101 sandite set 960994 alongside 101658 inside Longsite TMD on 9 August 1995.

DMBS 51426 from Class 101 set 101653 outside Longsite TMD in company with Scotrail and Network South East-liveried vehicles on 4 February 2001.

Left: An almost perfect line up (somebody please move the 156!) Longsite TMD on 5 February 2001. By this time, the arrival of the Scotrail units was obvious and brought some livery variety.

Below: **101682 is undergoing exam maintenance inside Longsite TMD on 4 February 2001.**

DMSL 51511 of ex-Scotrail Class 101 set 101689 is lifted on jacks for attention to its bogies in Longsite TMD on 4 February 2001. This vehicle has found its way into preservation at the North Yorkshire Moors Railway.

DMBS 53311 of Class 101 unit 101840 waits outside Longsite TMD on 4 February 2001. It was not uncommon in depots to split sets for maintenance, especially if lifting was to be involved.

Chapter 5
Storage and Disposal

The movement of scrap vehicles is often problematical. It is always preferable to move vehicles by rail where possible, but the length of time some are left standing idle often precludes this. By the time they were withdrawn, many Heritage DMUs were located in odd sidings having been dumped there following stripping for spares or some sort of failure, although more mobile vehicles may have left for preservation pastures or the scrapyard.

Many depots had been built without road access being considered, and moving an essentially immovable vehicle from the back of a remote siding to a location where it could be loaded was a major effort. A lot of persuasion and goodwill was sometimes needed, but as usual the professionalism of railwaymen and the specialist haulage companies prevailed and eventually vehicles were disposed of.

Happily, some further use was found for DMUs after withdrawal. Sometimes this was only to provide spares, but a number of vehicles were saved for preservation, some of them quite rare examples including the Class 119.

During the last years of operation, heavy maintenance was reduced to a level good enough to keep the units in safe operation. The development of the component exchange maintenance and Level 5 depot concept meant that a fair amount of work could be undertaken at the home depot.

In deepest Cornwall, Class 117 set 117304 was at St Blazey TMD on 13 April 1995 following damage sustained in a derailment a year before. After assessment on this visit, the vehicles were extracted by road and sent for preservation at the Plym Valley Railway, where they remain today.

Another out-of-service set in the West Country was 51399 at the famous depot of Plymouth Laira on 24 November 1994. This was not so lucky, as along with its mate, 51361, it was sent for scrap not long after this photo was taken.

Old Oak Common TMD was where most of the redundant Network South East DMUs were dumped. By this time a rarity on the network, Class 104 53477 and 53539 are seen on 17 January 1995. The Class 104 units last saw use on the Gospel Oak to Barking service before being replaced by Bletchley-based Class 117.

Above: Another Class 104 vehicle, DMBS 53450, at Old Oak Common depot on 17 January 1995. Sadly, none of the 104 vehicles seen here made it into preservation and were moved away by road for scrap. This in itself was quite an effort, as Old Oak Common is in a congested part of West London and there were a large amount of restrictions on the movement of loads of this size.

Left: My favourite class of DMU! I worked on them at Selhurst Depot and travelled on them when they operated the Gatwick Airport to Reading service, so I am happy to report that this vehicle, Class 119 DMBC 51074, made it into preservation and is currently at the Swindon and Cricklade Railway. It is seen at Old Oak Common TMD on 17 January 1995.

Another vehicle that was scrapped was Class 117 DMS 51414 at Old Oak Common in May 1995. Evidence of its use as a workforce carrier for use in the construction of the Channel Tunnel is visible. Quite a prestigious end to a long career.

Above: The Birmingham Cross-City line was electrified in 1993, but full service did not commence until late 1994. This meant that the hotch potch of DMU classes based at Tyseley TMD had to soldier on and just nudged into the privatisation era. The result was a virtual heaven for any DMUs fans, as four roads of Tyseley were dedicated to a massive variety of stored DMU vehicles, which were gradually whittled away for scrap and preservation. Class 119 51107 was not saved, however, the other Class 119 set at Tyseley, 51073 and 51104, was sent to the West Country and the delay gave time for it to be saved. The problem with Class 119s was the amount of blue asbestos they contained, which severely restricted their onward sale.

Right: Class 116 DMS 53823 stored at Tyseley Depot in February 1995.

Class 116 set T356 stored at Tyseley Depot in February 1995. Note the long-withdrawn Metro-Cammell Class 151 set stored out of service next to it. This was built as the company's proposal for a Heritage DMU replacement but lost out to what became the Class 150.

Class 121 55032 stored at Tyseley TMD in February 1995. This unit went on to be reinstated and used by Arriva on the Cardiff Bay branch. It is now preserved on the Wensleydale Railway.

This was the last survivor of Class 118; DMBS 51314 was stored at Tyseley Depot in February 1995. This was another vehicle that did not make it into preservation.

Class 101 vehicles 51444 and 54086 stored at Tyseley in February 1995.

Class 101 car 54220 demonstrates the difficulty of extracting withdrawn vehicles. Left behind when all its classmates were withdrawn, local staff worked hard in order to get vehicles to a position where they could be loaded on to a truck when it was finally ready for disposal. This is the situation at Norwich Crown Point on 21 December 1994.

Another location for storing units was Blackpool North. Aside from DMUs, a number of EMUs from the Manchester area were also stored here, a long time before wires were even installed. The purpose of our visit was to look at the Class 122s for possible use in the Cardiff Valleys, but unfortunately this was not to be. The leading unit is Class 122 55000 at Blackpool North, seen on 27 January 1996.

The Class 122 units ended up here following their stay of execution on the Cornish branches after the unsuccessful trial use of Pacers. Both units seen here at Blackpool North on 27 January 1996 happily made it into preservation, with 55000 going to the South Devon Railway and 55003 to the Gloucestershire Warwickshire Railway.

Class 101 set 101660 is stabled in Doncaster West Yard on 18 August 1995. The unit has just been released from Doncaster Works after attention. Units could often be seen here awaiting movement back to their home depots.

101842 with DMBS 53144 leading has just received attention at Doncaster Works on 31 March 1995 and is awaiting its journey back to Penzance. Later, in 1995, 101842 lost its trailer car 59110, which was sent for scrap.

In what appears to be someone's front garden, DTSL 54091 of Class 101 set 101658 is seen in Doncaster Works on 31 March 1995. This location was often used for official photographs of far grander traction than a common Metro Cammell Class 101 unit.

DMBS vehicle 51205 of Class 101 unit 101676 is seen at Doncaster Works on 31 March 1995. Corrosion was always a problem with Heritage DMU units throughout their lives, but luckily their construction was fairly simple and straightforward. Evidence of such repairs can be seen on the cab front of 51205.

Looking sparkling after a repaint inside Doncaster Works on 31 March 1995 is DMBS 51350 of North London set L701. This would be its last main overhaul before eventual withdrawal. One particular problem with Class 117s was corroded door pillars caused by rainwater ingress. This is still a major issue confronting preservationists today.

Chapter 6
Departmental Units

The usefulness of the Heritage DMUs was demonstrated by the number that ended up in departmental use following withdrawal. During the period covered by this book, there were several dotted around the network doing a variety of duties. This chapter shows those that I managed to catch up with in my travels and visits to depots.

The definition of a departmental unit is often very loose especially in the new world of privatisation, but could generally be described as a vehicle that had been taken out of revenue service and is now in use for some further task in the operation of the railway and is often specifically modified for this task.

Right: Following the takeover by Networker Turbo units in 1993, Reading TMD was left with a few Class 121 single-car units acting as sandite vehicles to remind of days past. 977722 (ex-55020) is seen at Reading TMD on 1 May 1998. This unit went on to become one of the last Heritage units in service as, after transfer to Aylesbury TMD, Chiltern Railway rebuilt and reinstated it into mainline service to operate the Aylesbury to Princes Risborough line. It was finally withdrawn in 2017 and is now preserved at the Bodmin & Wenford Railway.

Below: Class 121 977860 (ex-55022) at Princes Risborough on 29 October 1999. This was operating as a sandite vehicle based out of Aylesbury. This was one of the few Class 121 units that did not survive into preservation.

Above: Class 121 9778858 (ex-55024) at Aylesbury TMD on 7 March 1999. This vehicle was painted in a unique London, Midland and Scottish Railway-inspired livery, which it has retained after entering preservation and being restored to passenger service at the Chinnor & Princes Risborough Railway.

Left: Class 121 960012 (ex-55028) at Aylesbury Depot on 28 October 1999. Following the end of its use at Aylesbury, it found its way into preservation at the Swanage Railway where it has been completely restored to passenger use.

Class 122 975042 (ex-55019) Stratford Low Level on a crew training trip on 22 September 1995. This vehicle had quite a short time in mainline service, being built by Gloucester Railway Carriage and Wagon Company in 1958 and taken into departmental use as a route learning unit in 1970. Anyone standing at this spot today would find the scene unrecognisable following the complete rebuild of Stratford station.

Above: Class 122 975042 (ex-55019) at Bletchley TMD on 3 February 2000. It is now in Railtrack livery and in use as a sandite vehicle. It went into preservation in 2014 and is currently at the Llanelli & Mynydd Mawr Railway.

Right: Class 122 55012 never carried its allocated departmental number of 977941, but it was transferred to freight operator Loadhaul in 1994 and painted in its colours. It was based at Thornaby TMD. It has survived in preservation and is currently in operation at the Weardale Railway Trust. It is seen at Derby on 11 May 1999.

Class 101 sandite set 960993 (977899 is ex-51427, and 977900 is ex-50321) at Longsite TMD on 9 August 1995. A number of Class 101 sets were converted into the dual role of sandite and Route Learner units and based at Longsite. 50321 from this set has been preserved on the Great Central Railway.

Class 101 sandite set 960991 (977901 is ex-50200 and 977900 is ex-50231) at Longsite TMD on 9 May 2000. The sandite duties involved laying an adhesion aid in the autumn leaf fall season to assist with wheelslip and slide problems.

Class 101 sandite set 960994 (977895 is ex-50308 and 977896 is ex-50331) at Longsite TMD on 9 May 2000. Upon privatisation, the sandite units came under the control of Railtrack. Interestingly, the sandite units based at Longsite were withdrawn a few years before the end of passenger operation.

We have seen Class 101 set 101842 before in Cornwall. After its use finished there, it was acquired by SERCO and painted in its distinctive livery. It was used as a tractor unit for moving vehicles around. It only lasted a couple of years in this guise before going for scrap in late 1999. It is seen outside Derby RTC from a passing HST on 27 September 1999. Nowadays, vehicles at this location would be a sea of Network Rail yellow.

Class 101 DTCL 56342 at Neville Hill TMD December 2001. This vehicle spent some time tucked away around the back of the multiple unit depot. The vehicle was withdrawn in 1989 and was used as a store until sold into preservation in 2005. It currently resides with the Great Central Railway.

Other books you might like:

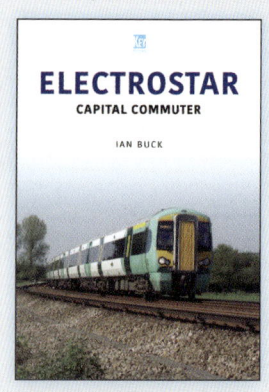

ELECTROSTAR
CAPITAL COMMUTER
IAN BUCK
Britain's Railways Series, Vol. 48

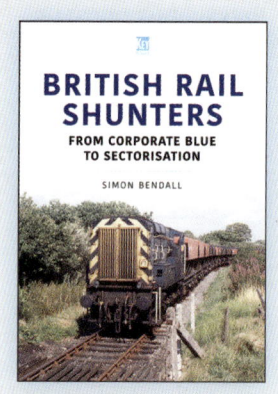

BRITISH RAIL SHUNTERS
FROM CORPORATE BLUE TO SECTORISATION
SIMON BENDALL
Britain's Railways Series, Vol. 46

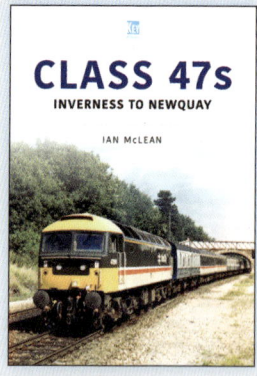

CLASS 47s
INVERNESS TO NEWQUAY
IAN McLEAN
Britain's Railways Series, Vol. 38

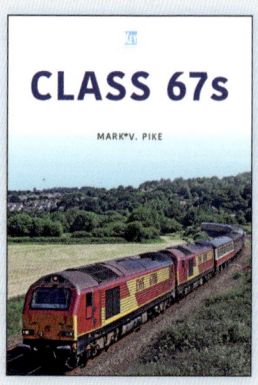

CLASS 67s
MARK V. PIKE
Britain's Railways Series, Vol. 30

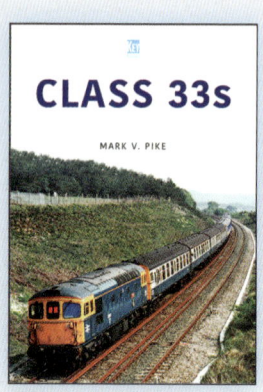

CLASS 33s
MARK V. PIKE
Britain's Railways Series, Vol. 40

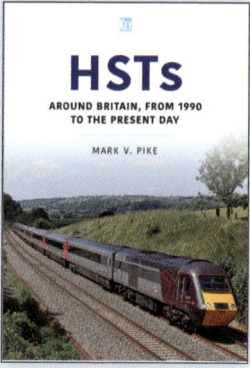

HSTs
AROUND BRITAIN, FROM 1990 TO THE PRESENT DAY
MARK V. PIKE
Britain's Railways Series, Vol. 33

For our full range of titles please visit:
shop.keypublishing.com/books

VIP Book Club

Sign up today and receive
TWO FREE E-BOOKS

Be the first to find out about our forthcoming book releases and receive exclusive offers.

Register now at **keypublishing.com/vip-book-club**

Our VIP Book Club is a 100% spam-free zone, and we will never share your email with anyone else. You can read our full privacy policy at: privacy.keypublishing.com